Bryan Chapman Bowers

THE WEALTH MASTERY

Building A Solid Financial Framework And
Creating Wealth Through Innovation

BRYAN CHAPMAN BOWERS

Bryan Chapman Bowers

Copyright©2024 Bryan Chapman Bowers

All Right Reserved

INTRODUCTION	**7**
CHAPTER ONE	**13**
GOAL-SETTING WITH MONEY	13
CHAPTER TWO	**20**
FINANCIAL PLANNING AND BUDGETING	20
CHAPTER THREE	**27**
TECHNIQUES FOR HANDLING DEBT	27
CHAPTER FOUR	**36**
PRINCIPLES OF INVESTING	36
CHAPTER FIVE	**44**
SOURCE OF INCOME	44
CHAPTER SIX	**52**
WEALTH FROM REAL ESTATE	52
CHAPTER SEVEN	**59**

MAKING PLANS FOR RETIREMENT	**59**
CHAPTER EIGHT	**67**
TAX STRATEGIES	**67**
CHAPTER NINE	**73**
SAFEGUARDING AND PRESERVING WEALTH	**73**
CHAPTER TEN	**79**
ONGOING EDUCATION AND ADJUSTMENT	**79**
CHAPTER ELEVEN	**85**
CONCLUSION	**85**

Bryan Chapman Bowers

INTRODUCTION

Welcome to the book "Wealth Mastery: A Comprehensive Guide to Building Prosperity." We will examine the ideas, methods, and frame of mind required to create long-term prosperity and attain financial plenty on this enlightening trip. This book is intended to provide you with the information and resources you need to successfully navigate the complex world of wealth creation, regardless of where you are in your wealth-building path or how you want to strengthen your current financial foundation.

What Constitutes Wealth

For you, what does riches mean? Gaining a firm idea of what wealth means to you is essential before diving into plans and techniques. Wealth is more than just money; it's the ability to follow your passions, take care of your family, and make a significant contribution to your society. We shall redefine wealth throughout this guide as a comprehensive idea that combines material success with personal fulfillment and social influence.

The Value of Financial Knowledge

The foundation of any successful wealth-building endeavor is financial knowledge. We will stress the need of developing a strong grasp of financial concepts in this part. A comprehensive financial education is essential for making well-informed decisions and navigating the intricacies of the financial environment, from investing and budgeting to managing debt and tax laws.

A Change in Attitude: Fostering a Wealth-Building Mentality
Beyond useful tactics, your success in the financial world greatly depends on the mentality you

adopt. Developing perseverance in the face of failures, accepting obstacles as opportunities, and adopting a growth mentality are all components of cultivating a wealth-building attitude. This change in perspective is the starting point for a profound transformation that will enable you to get through challenges and maintain your concentration on your path to success.

Remember that creating money is a journey rather than a goal as we set out on our examination of wealth mastery. our path calls for commitment, never-ending learning, and a proactive attitude to financial well-being. Whether your goals are to leave a legacy, become financially independent, or just have more control over your financial destiny, "Wealth Mastery" is your all-inclusive manual for making dreams come true. Together, let's set off on the path to long-term success and financial empowerment.

Bryan Chapman Bowers

CHAPTER ONE

Goal-Setting with Money

Achieving financial mastery begins with defining specific, attainable goals. We will explore how to develop SMART goals, make a vision board, and define both short- and long-term goals in this chapter. All of these strategies will help you achieve financial success.

Determining Both Short- and Long-Term Goals

1. Realizing the Significance of Objectives:
 • Examine why establishing financial objectives is essential to

accumulating money.
- Be aware of how motivation and attention are affected by well-defined objectives.

2. Short-term Financial Goals: Establish clear, precise goals for your finances. Some examples include setting up an emergency fund, paying off high-interest debt, or setting aside money for a certain item.

3. Long-Term Financial Goals:
- Visualize the kind of financial future you want.
- Establish long-term objectives, such as saving for retirement, buying a home, or paying for

schooling.

4. Goal Alignment with Values: Make sure your financial objectives are in line with your values and life goals.
- Commitment and fulfillment are increased when your goals and values align harmoniously.

SMART Goal-Setting 1. Particular Objectives:
- Be specific and clear in defining your financial objectives.
- Clearly state your goals and the reasons behind them.

2. Measurable Progress: • Create quantifiable standards by which to

gauge advancement.
- Divide more ambitious objectives into more manageable checkpoints.

3. Achievable Goals: • Evaluate whether your objectives are realistic.
- Make sure your goals are difficult yet doable with hard work and dedication.

4. Relevant Objectives: • Match every objective to your overall financial strategy.
- Determine if the objective significantly advances your overall quest to accumulate riches.

5. Time-Bound Objectives: Establish deadlines for each goal's

completion.
- Time-bound objectives assist focus work and create a sense of urgency.

Making a Financial Success Vision Board

1. Visualization and Manifestation: Recognize the role that visualization plays in helping people succeed financially.
- Examine how making a vision board might help you to visualize your objectives.

2. Gathering Visual Elements: Gather pictures, sayings, and symbols that symbolize your goals in terms of money.

- Your vision board's visual story will be composed of these components.

3. Setting Up Your Vision Board: • Organize the images on a board or in an electronic file.

- Design a layout that suits your tastes and personal style.

4. Consistent Reflection and Modification: • Schedule frequent reflection time for your vision board.

- Update and modify it as new objectives or desires arise.

Establishing financial objectives serves as a compass for constructing wealth. You build a purpose-driven and targeted approach to financial success by defining your short- and long-term goals, learning how to construct SMART goals, and making a vision board. As we go, keep in mind that these objectives are not just final destinations; rather, they are the turning points that mold your journey toward enduring wealth.

Bryan Chapman Bowers

CHAPTER TWO

Financial Planning and Budgeting

A strong financial foundation is based on financial planning and budgeting. This chapter will cover the fundamentals of financial success, the craft of crafting a workable budget, and the significance of setting aside money for emergencies and saves.

The Basis for Monetary Achievement
1. Comprehending Financial Well-Being: • Describe what financial well-being is and how important it

is to you.
- Understand how financial security and general life satisfaction are related.

2. Financial Awareness: • Get a clear understanding of your present financial circumstances.
- To get a whole picture, assess revenue, costs, assets, and liabilities.

3. Goal Alignment: • Match your life's general aims with your financial aspirations.
- Motivation is increased when your personal and financial goals are in harmony.

4. Constant Learning: Adopt a mindset that views financial concerns as a never-ending source of learning.
- Keep up with market developments, investment possibilities, and personal finance tactics.

Establishing a Reasonable Budget

1. Income Assessment: Consider every source of revenue.
- Make sure you comprehend your net income after all applicable taxes and deductions.

2. Expense Categorization: Sort expenses into groups that are fixed and variables.

- Determine what expenses are not negotiable, such as rent or a mortgage, as well as extravagance.

3. SMART Budgeting:
- When creating a budget, use SMART guidelines.
- Establish time-bound, meaningful, quantifiable, realistic, and detailed goals for every area of expenses.

4. Tracking and Monitoring:
- Make use of applications and budgeting tools to keep tabs on your spending.
- Keep a close eye on your expenditures to spot areas that might want improvement.

Increasing Your Savings and

Emergency Funds

1. The Significance of an Emergency Fund: Recognize the vital part an emergency fund plays in maintaining financial security.
• See it as a safety net against unforeseen costs or drops in income.

2. Deciding on the Amount of the Emergency Fund: • Figure out how much money you should set aside for emergencies.
• Aim for a living expenditure cushion of three to six months in case of unanticipated events.

3. Savings Techniques: • Examine several techniques for saving, such

as the 50/30/20 rule.

• Set aside a percentage of your money for savings, goals, and needs.

4. Automated Savings: • Configure your savings accounts to receive automatic transfers.

• Savings that are automated are consistent and less enticing to spend.

The foundations of financial success are financial planning and budgeting, which offer the structure and discipline required to accumulate money. You lay the groundwork for resilience and long-term prosperity by having a clear awareness of your financial status, making a realistic budget, and giving emergency and savings money priority. As we move forward, remember that a carefully thought-out financial plan serves as a foundation for accomplishing your long-term financial objectives in addition to meeting your immediate requirements.

Bryan Chapman Bowers

CHAPTER THREE

Techniques for Handling Debt

Achieving financial success mostly depends on managing and getting rid of debt. This chapter is devoted to helping you comprehend the many forms of debt, develop a smart strategy for repaying it, and implement preventative measures to keep from taking on more debt.

Recognizing Various Debt Types

1. Good Debt vs. Bad Debt: Distinguish between "good" debts that advance long-term objectives and "bad" loans that impede financial advancement.

- High-interest credit card debt is an example of bad debt, whereas mortgages are an example of good debt.

2. Secured vs. Unsecured Debt: Examine the differences between debt that is secured by collateral and debt that is unsecured (not secured by any particular asset).
- Recognize the effects of default on various debt kinds.

Fixed vs. Variable Interest Rates: Know how your debt is affected by both fixed and variable interest rates.
- Understand how changes in interest rates may affect your

whole repayment plan.

4. Prioritizing High-Interest Debt: Create a strategy to pay off high-interest debt first in order to minimize interest payments. Give higher-interest debt priority.

Making a Plan to Pay Off Debt

Obtaining Debt Information: This is the first step in developing a successful repayment plan. It entails compiling a thorough list of all obligations, including interest rates, minimum payments, and outstanding sums.

• This is the starting point for developing a successful repayment plan.

2. Snowball vs. Avalanche Methods:
- Examine well-liked debt payback techniques including the debt avalanche and snowball methods.
- Select a strategy that fits both your psychological and financial inclinations.

3. talking with Creditors: Managing debt arrangements can result from effective communication and negotiation. Take into account talking with creditors for more advantageous payback terms or reduced interest rates.

4. Debt Consolidation alternatives: Assess your alternatives for consolidating debt, including

moving amounts to a loan with a reduced interest rate or combining many loans into one.

• Recognize the possible advantages and disadvantages of consolidating your debt.

• Recognize the possible advantages and disadvantages of consolidating your debt.

Techniques for Preventing the Acquisition of Superfluous Debt

1. Budgeting for anticipated needs: To reduce your dependency on credit, set aside money in your budget for anticipated needs.

• Plan ahead and save money for

important purchases to prevent debt accumulation.

2. Maintenance of Emergency reserve: Keep a sizeable emergency reserve on hand to pay for unforeseen costs.

Why Having emergency funds lowers the likelihood that unanticipated events may need the use of credit cards.

3. Critical Assessment of Needs vs. Wants: • Grow an astute perspective while making this distinction.

• Set needs first to avoid accruing debt for non-essential purchases.

4. Credit Card Discipline: Refrain

from making needless expenditures and use credit cards sensibly.

Pay off credit card debt in full each month to avoid interest building up.

One essential component of reaching financial freedom is managing your debt. You may go a long way toward laying a solid financial foundation by being aware of the many kinds of debt, developing a smart repayment plan, and taking proactive steps to stay out of debt. As we move forward, keep in mind that good debt management involves both getting rid of current obligations and developing a way of thinking that keeps debt from building up in the future.

CHAPTER FOUR
Principles of Investing

A major component of accumulating money is investing, and long-term financial success depends on having a solid knowledge of basic investing concepts. This chapter covers the fundamentals of risk management and diversification, gives an overview of stocks, bonds, and real estate, and highlights the significance of assembling a well-balanced investment portfolio.

Risk management and diversification.

1. Gain an understanding of diversification: 1. Examine diversity as a risk management technique. 2. Learn how investing in a variety of asset classes can reduce market volatility-related risks.

2. Asset Class Diversification: • Spread your holdings over a range of asset classes, such as bonds, equities, property, and other financial instruments.
• Examine the risk-return characteristics of various assets to build a portfolio that is well-rounded.

3. Sector and Geographic diversity:
• Expand diversity to include

industrial sectors and geographic areas in addition to asset types.

• Lessen exposure to certain economic hazards related to a given area or industry.

4. Risk Assessment of Tolerance:

• Assess your investing horizon and risk tolerance.

• Align your portfolio with your financial objectives and preferred level of risk.

Overview of Bonds, Stocks, and Real Estate

1. Stocks (Equities): Recognize the fundamentals of stocks as ownership stakes in a business.

• Learn about various stock kinds,

such as ordinary and preferred stocks.

2. Bonds (Fixed-Income Securities):

- Understand what bonds are as financial products.
- Acquire knowledge of the connection between yield, interest rates, and bond prices.

3. Real Estate Investing: Examine real estate as a possible avenue for investing.

- Recognize the advantages and disadvantages of purchasing real estate or real estate investment trusts (REITs).

4. Risk and Return Profiles: Examine how stocks, bonds, and real estate

have different risk and return characteristics.

• Take into account the relative contributions of each asset type to the overall diversification of your portfolio.

Putting Together a Well-Balanced Investment Portfolio

1. Strategies for Allocating a Portfolio: Examine several approaches, such as the 60/40 (stocks/bonds) guideline.

• Adjust the allocation of your portfolio to reflect your time horizon, risk tolerance, and financial goals.

2. Frequent Portfolio Rebalancing: • Adopt a methodical strategy for doing regular portfolio rebalancing.
• Make sure that over time, your asset allocation sticks to your investment plan.
3. Periodic Risk Assessment: Evaluate your investment portfolio on a regular basis for risks.
• As your financial circumstances and risk tolerance change, modify the amount of risk exposure in your portfolio.
4. Professional Guidance: Take into account consulting investment advisors or other financial experts for assistance.

- Make the most of their knowledge to maximize your investing approach and make wise judgments.

A thorough grasp of risk management, diversification, and the properties of various asset types is necessary for prudent investment. Adopting these investment tenets and creating a well-balanced portfolio puts you in a position to succeed financially in the long run. As we move forward, keep in mind that building wealth and ensuring financial stability are largely dependent on a well-structured and diversified investment strategy.

CHAPTER FIVE

Source of Income

One of the most important strategies for accumulating money and succeeding financially is to have several sources of income. This chapter will cover side projects and entrepreneurship, as well as tactics for optimizing your earning potential in the workplace. It will also cover the fundamentals of leveraging numerous revenue sources.

Utilizing Various Revenue Sources
1. Gaining an Understanding of

various Income Streams: Examine the idea of having various sources of income and how it contributes to financial stability.
- Be aware of the advantages of having a variety of sources of income.

2. Finding Possible revenue Streams: To find possible sources of revenue, evaluate your abilities, hobbies, and capabilities.
- Take into account passive revenue streams like royalties or investments.

3. Equilibrium of Active and Passive Revenue:
- Achieve equilibrium between

active income, which is obtained by your own efforts, and passive income, which is obtained with little to no work or active participation.

- Look into real estate, internet businesses, and investment alternatives for passive income.

Examining Side Projects and Entrepreneurship

1. The Entrepreneurial Mindset: Recognize the mentality needed to pursue business.

- Value traits like imagination, fortitude, and a readiness to take measured chances.

2. Finding Entrepreneurial Opportunities: Investigate possible

ventures that complement your interests and abilities.
- Examine market trends and needs to find chances for successful entrepreneurship.

3. Launching a Side Business: Investigate the idea of side businesses as a means of making extra money.
- Pick side projects that go well with your abilities and those you can work on in addition to your primary source of income.

4. Juggling Work and Side Projects:
- Create efficient time management techniques to maintain a healthy work-life balance while juggling side

projects.
- Make sure your side projects contribute to your overall wellbeing rather than detracting from it.

Optimizing Your Career's Earning Potential

1. Continuous Skill Development: To remain competitive in your field, make an investment in ongoing education and skill development.
- Recognize new trends and pick up pertinent skills to increase your worth in the work place.

2. Bargaining for Increased Salary:
- Get skilled at negotiating to push for greater pay.
- Study industry norms and be

ready to explain your worth to potential employers.

3. Looking for prospects for Career progression: • Within your present company, actively look for prospects for career progression.
• Discuss your professional objectives with managers and look at opportunities for advancement.
4. Networking and Mentoring: To get job possibilities and assistance, establish a robust professional network.
• Look for mentoring from seasoned people who can offer insightful commentary and

guidance.

Essential tactics for generating revenue include investigating entrepreneurship and side hustles, diversifying your sources of income through numerous streams, and optimizing your earning potential within your employment. You may establish a strong financial foundation that supports your objectives and desires by taking an entrepreneurial and proactive approach to life. As we go, keep in mind that generating revenue involves more than just quantity; it also involves strategically coordinating your efforts to produce significant and long-term financial progress.

CHAPTER SIX

Wealth from Real Estate

For a very long time, real estate has been essential to building wealth. This chapter will cover the principles of real estate investment, tactics for buying a property, and efficient ways to maintain and increase your real estate holdings.

An Overview of Investing in Real Estate

1. Comprehending Real Estate as an Investment: • Examine the benefits of real estate as a category of investments.

• Be aware of the possibilities for

portfolio diversification, passive income, and long-term appreciation.

2. Kinds of Investments in Real Estate:

• Explore a range of real estate investment opportunities, such as rental, commercial, and residential properties.

• Recognize the special qualities and possible profits of each kind.

3. Real Estate Risk and Return:

• Evaluate the dangers of making real estate investments.

• Take prospective benefits into account.

- Take into account variables including property quality, location, and market trends while evaluating possible benefits.

Techniques for Purchasing Real Estate

1. Establishing investing Goals: 1. Clearly state your overall financial objectives in terms of your investing goals.
- Choose whether you want to concentrate on property appreciation, rental revenue, or both.

2. Market Research and Analysis: To find attractive locations and possible development regions, do

in-depth market research.
• Examine economic statistics, real estate valuations, and market trends.
3. Financing Strategies: • Examine various forms of funding, such as loans, partnerships, and mortgages.
• Determine the best financing plan for your objectives in terms of investments and financial status.
4. Due Diligence in home Selection:
• Before purchasing a home, carry out thorough due diligence.
• Take into account elements including the state of the property, prospective upgrades, and the possibility for neighborhood

expansion.

Taking Care of and Expanding Property Holdings

1. Effective Property Management: Create a solid plan for managing your property.

Depending on your tastes and available funds, think about managing your property yourself or through an outsourced company.

2. Optimizing Rental Revenue

- Put methods into place to optimize rental income, such maintaining appealing features and establishing competitive rents.
- For more freedom, look at short-

term renting choices.

3. Property Appreciation and Improvements: To increase value, make improvements and modifications to your property.

- Keep abreast of market developments and give priority to upgrades that suit the tastes of prospective tenants or buyers.

4. Scaling Your Real Estate Portfolio: Investigate ways to grow your portfolio gradually.

- Take into account strategically buying more properties, leveraging equity, or reinvesting earnings.

When used correctly, real estate wealth may be a potent tool for financial advancement. You may construct a solid real estate portfolio that supports your wealth-building objectives by grasping the principles of real estate investment, using practical methods for acquiring properties, and putting good management techniques into place.

As we go, keep in mind that real estate investing involves more than just buying and selling properties—it also entails making wise choices that will lead to sustained financial success.

CHAPTER SEVEN

Making Plans for Retirement

Making plans for your retirement is essential to safeguarding your financial future. This chapter will cover the fundamentals of retirement accounts, retirement-specific investing methods that work, and the idea of planning for financial independence in general.

Comprehending Retirement Accounts

1. Retirement Account Types:

• Examine popular retirement accounts, such as pension plans, IRAs, Roth IRAs, and 401(k)s.

- Recognize the special characteristics, tax ramifications, and contribution caps of every account.

2. Employer-Sponsored Retirement Plans: Acquaint yourself with the nuances of plans offered by employers.

- Examine the advantages of rollover choices, vesting schedules, and employer contributions.

3. IRAs, or individual retirement accounts:

Examine the tax benefits and adaptability of individual retirement accounts.

- Evaluate Traditional and Roth IRAs to see which is a better fit for your situation.

Retirement Investment Strategies

1. Asset Allocation and Risk Tolerance:
- Determine your level of risk tolerance and match it to a sensible asset allocation plan.
- Recognize how diverse portfolios help to minimize risk and maximize rewards.

2. Dollar-Cost Averaging: Examine how this strategy can help with long-term retirement investment.
- Use systematic contributions to investments to lessen the effects of

market volatility.

3. Rebalancing Your Portfolio: • Create a plan for how often to adjust the investments in your portfolio.

• Make sure your asset allocation stays in accordance with your time horizon for retirement and risk tolerance.

4. Income Generation in Retirement: Establish a strategy for bringing in money in retirement by combining investment withdrawals, Social Security, and pensions.

• Investigate realistic withdrawal rates to preserve your financial stability in retirement.

Putting Financial Independence Plans in Place

1. What is meant by financial independence?

- Clearly define what you mean by financial freedom and how it will affect your retirement.
- Take into account non-financial considerations including lifestyle decisions and personal contentment.

2. Emergency reserves in Retirement: To pay for unforeseen expenditures, save emergency reserves even after retiring.

- Make sure you have money set up for unanticipated medical expenses or house maintenance.

3. Long-Term Care and Insurance: Examine your alternatives for long-term care insurance and how they fit into your overall retirement strategy.

- Evaluate how possible medical expenses may affect your retirement funds.

4. Legacy Planning and Estate Management: Take into account the distribution of assets to heirs as well as legacy planning.

- Learn about beneficiary designations, trusts, and wills as estate management instruments.

Retirement planning is about building a road map for achieving financial independence and leading a satisfying life, not merely getting ready for the end of your work. You may confidently negotiate the challenges of retirement by being aware of retirement accounts, putting good investing techniques into practice, and making plans for longer-term financial independence. As we go, keep in mind that retirement is a dynamic stage of life, and careful preparation guarantees that you will not only leave anything behind but also live a life that fulfills your goals and desires.

CHAPTER EIGHT

Tax Strategies

One of the most important components of constructing wealth is tax management. This chapter will cover ways to optimize tax efficiency, take advantage of credits and deductions, and discuss the value of consulting a tax expert.

Increasing Tax Efficiency

1. Gaining Knowledge on Tax Efficiency

- Describe tax efficiency and how it affects your entire financial plan.
- Understand that reducing tax obligations is essential to

maximizing wealth.

2. Planning for Strategic Income:
- Investigate methods for handling taxable income.
- To maximize tax results, take into account income deferral, tax-efficient investments, and timing techniques.

3. Tax-Efficient Investments: Invest in assets like long-term capital gains that have a favorable tax treatment.
- Look into investing instruments that minimize taxes, such as tax-managed funds and index funds.

Wealth Builder Tax Credits and Deductions

1. Typical Tax Benefits for Wealth Creators:
• Determine which important deductions apply to wealth creators.
• Examine the deductions available for charity contributions, school costs, and mortgage interest.

2. Wealth Builder Tax Credits: Recognize the tax credits that are available to you since they can immediately lower your tax obligation.
• Examine credits for childcare, energy efficiency, and education.

3. Retirement Account Contributions: For both immediate

and long-term tax benefits, increase your retirement account contributions to the maximum extent possible.

• Recognize how contributions to standard and Roth retirement accounts affect your taxes.

Using Tax Professionals

1. The Function of Enrolled Agents:

• Recognize the advantages of collaborating with tax experts.

• Appreciate the knowledge that tax experts provide to tax strategies, compliance, and planning.

2. Selecting the Correct Tax Professional: • Look into various tax

specialists, such as tax attorneys and Certified Public Accountants (CPAs).

- Pick an expert whose knowledge matches your objectives and financial status.

3. Year-Round Tax Planning: To optimize advantages, embrace year-round tax planning.

- Work with tax experts outside of tax season to put preventative measures into action.

4. Audit assistance and Representation: Take into account tax experts who provide services for audit assistance and representation.

- Recognize the value of expert support in the event of a tax audit.

Effective wealth-building tactics include maximizing tax efficiency, utilizing credits and deductions, and consulting with tax experts. Through proactive tax preparation and using expert knowledge, you may maximize your financial results and protect a larger portion of your hard-earned money. As we go, keep in mind that smart tax management is crucial to achieving financial stability and success—it's not simply about complying with regulations.

Bryan Chapman Bowers

CHAPTER NINE

Safeguarding and Preserving Wealth

Building money is not as important as safeguarding and preserving it. This chapter will cover asset protection techniques, the fundamentals of estate planning, and the function of insurance in wealth preservation.

Essentials of Estate Planning

1. Comprehend Estate Planning: • Describe estate planning and its role in protecting wealth.

• Be aware of the overarching

objectives, such as legacy planning, tax efficiency, and asset distribution.

2. Estate Planning Elements: • Examine essential elements such powers of attorney, trusts, and wills.

• Recognize the function of guardianship agreements and healthcare directives.

3. Reducing Estate Taxes: • Put mechanisms into place to reduce estate taxes.

• Look at tax-efficient arrangements such as charity contributions and marriage trusts. Techniques for Asset Protection

1. Establishing Legal Structures: To safeguard assets, investigate legal structures such family limited partnerships (FLPs) and limited liability organizations (LLCs).
- Recognize how these arrangements might protect assets from possible threats.

2. Asset Diversification: Stress the need of asset diversification in reducing risk.
- To lessen exposure, stay away from over-concentration in a particular asset type.

3. Homestead Exemptions: Recognize the protection that homestead exemptions provide for

principal dwellings.
- Look into laws that protect the principal house from certain creditors.

Insurance to Preserve Wealth

1. Strategies for Life Insurance: Examine life insurance as a means of preserving money.
- Recognize the ways in which life insurance might cover income replacement or estate taxes.

2. Long-Term Care Insurance: Evaluate how crucial long-term care insurance is to preserving wealth.
- Understand how assets can be shielded from the high cost of healthcare by this insurance.

3. Liability Insurance: Make sure you have the right kind of coverage.
• Assess if umbrella insurance are required to offer extra security above and beyond basic coverage.

4. Insurance Policy Reviews and Updates: • Examine insurance plans on a regular basis.
• Verify that the coverage fits your lifestyle, assets, and current financial condition lifestyle and assets portfolio.

Preserving and safeguarding your wealth is essential to guaranteeing the duration and influence of your financial inheritance. You may strengthen your financial foundation against unanticipated obstacles by applying asset protection techniques, employing insurance judiciously, and incorporating basics of estate planning. As we go, keep in mind that wealth preservation is about building a strong financial framework that can endure uncertainty and the test of time while having a long-lasting effect on future generations.

CHAPTER TEN

Ongoing Education and Adjustment

The path to financial success is a dynamic and always changing one. In order to succeed continuously, we will discuss in this last chapter the significance of maintaining knowledge of financial markets, adopting a growth mentality, and adjusting to shifts in the economy.

Keeping Up With The Financial Markets

1. Market Awareness: Acknowledge the value of maintaining up to date knowledge of the financial markets.

- Keep a close eye on world events, economic data, and market developments that may have an influence on your financial portfolio.

2. Financial News and Resources: Look into reliable sources and resources for financial news.

- To improve your comprehension of market dynamics, make use of financial magazines, internet resources, and professional analysis.

3. Professional guidance: It is advisable to consult with recognized specialists for professional financial guidance.

- Consult financial experts that are able to offer individualized insights based on your goal and risk tolerance.

Adopting a Growth Perspective

1. Fostering an Attitude of Growth:

- Recognize the idea of a growth mindset in relation to achieving financial success. • Accept obstacles as chances to learn and see failures as opportunities to get better.

2. Ongoing Education: Make a commitment to ongoing financial education.

- To increase your understanding and proficiency in wealth-building techniques, participate in webinars, seminars, and workshops.

3. Learning from Mistakes: • Have a positive outlook on errors and disappointments.

- Examine poor financial choices to glean insightful knowledge for next advancements.

Long-term financial success is built on a foundation of constant learning and adaptability. You may position yourself as a resilient and proactive wealth creator by maintaining financial market knowledge, adopting a growth mentality, and making adjustments in response to shifting economic conditions. As we get to the end of this tutorial, keep in mind that achieving financial success is a lifetime process that requires learning, adjusting, and growing. In your financial path, embrace the obstacles, acknowledge your successes, and never stop trying to do better.

Bryan Chapman Bowers

CHAPTER ELEVEN

Conclusion

With "Wealth Mastery: A Comprehensive Guide to Financial Success" reaches its completion, congratulations! You now have the information and techniques necessary to start a profitable wealth-building journey thanks to this guide. As you digest the abundance of information that has been provided, keep the following important points in mind:

Honoring Financial Achievements Recognize and appreciate all of your financial accomplishments, no matter how large or small. Every achievement you've had, no matter if it's debt repayment, investing objectives met, or first-time home ownership, is evidence of your commitment and discipline. Honoring these achievements encourages you to aim for even greater financial success and strengthens your optimistic outlook.

Transferring Wealth: Making a Legacy

It's critical to think about the legacy you wish to leave behind as you accumulate riches. Legacy planning is carefully analyzing the potential effects of your wealth on future generations. You may leave a lasting legacy through charity giving, estate planning, or imparting financial knowledge to future generations. Spend some time explaining your goals and ideals around how your riches will affect your family, community and causes you care about.

Encouragement to Keep Creating Wealth

Achieving financial success is a continuous process. Accept the lessons you've learned, adjust to your environment, and don't waver from your financial objectives.

Always look for ways to improve your wealth-building tactics and your understanding of finance. Recall that obstacles are opportunities to grow and learn, and that failures are only temporary.

Concluding Remarks of Motivation

Building wealth is about establishing a life of stability, fulfillment, and purpose rather than just making money. Your tenacity, fortitude, and dedication to a better future are reflected in your financial achievement. As you go, remember your financial values, keep an open mind to new possibilities, and put your health first at all times.

We appreciate you devoting time and effort to "Wealth Mastery." I hope and pray that your financial path brings you wealth, success, and the ability to achieve your biggest goals. Continue accumulating the riches you merit!